Dating
Decisions

A 4-week course to help senior highers discover how their Christian values apply to dating

by David Cassady

Group
Loveland, Colorado

Dating Decisions
Copyright © 1991 by Group Publishing, Inc.

Credits
Edited by Stephen Parolini
Cover designed by Jill Christopher and DeWain Stoll
Interior designed by Judy Bienick and Jan Aufdemberge
Illustrations by Raymond Medici

14   13   12   11   10   9   8   7   04   03   02   01   00   99   98   97

ISBN 1-55945-215-3
Printed in the United States of America.

CONTENTS

INTRODUCTION 4

Dating Decisions

COURSE OBJECTIVES.....................5

HOW TO USE THIS COURSE............6

THIS COURSE AT A GLANCE............8

PUBLICITY PAGE 9

LESSON 1.....................................11

Why Date?

Help senior highers form positive images and motives for dating.

LESSON 2.....................................22

Is It Love?

Help senior highers gain a deeper understanding of what it means to love.

LESSON 3.....................................30

Dating and Sex

Help senior highers base decisions about dating and sex on Christian values.

LESSON 4.....................................38

Breaking Up Is Hard to Do

Help senior highers discover healthy ways to deal with the painful endings of romantic relationships.

BONUS IDEAS 45

DATING DECISIONS

H is heart pounded so loudly he felt sure it sounded like a bass drum to everyone around him. But this time he was going to do it—he was going to end the useless speculation and worry. Would she go out with him? Or just slam the locker door and explode with laughter?

Putting those thoughts behind him, Jeff turned down the hall. Today he was going to ask Beth out for a date.

• • •

Anyone who's ever dated can remember the intense emotions that preceded a date and usually continued for most of the date. All the self-esteem and identity you mustered were placed on the line for the date.

Today it's not much different.

Why all the pressure? Kids are in the midst of the most gut-wrenching period of their lives when it comes to knowing who they are. They search for identity in clothing, music, tennis-shoe brand names, cars and the kinds of people they spend time with.

Dating intensifies the self-identity struggle. A teenager on a date is focused more on finding approval from the other person than on anything else. And kids get into all kinds of trouble (such as sexual activities) trying to gain that approval.

The face of dating is constantly changing. But old questions continue to plague love-sick teenagers. How can teenagers find what it means to love? How can they discover healthy ways of relating and even breaking up?

The church can help teenagers form a healthy self-image and an identity rooted in Christian values. If we help kids see the real-world common sense in these values, they'll be more likely to live by them. Jesus didn't teach things like "sex is meant for marriage" just for fun, but

Dating and Teenagers

- 70 percent of teenagers date.
- 71 percent of teenagers say they've been in love.
- 50 percent of high school seniors date at least once a week.
- 77 percent of teenage girls believe a good personality is the most important consideration in choosing who to date.
- 64 percent of teenage guys would turn down an offer to date because the girl isn't pretty.
- More than 80 percent of teenagers would date someone despite their parents' objections.

because it makes sense to intimately reveal oneself only in a setting of commitment and acceptance of responsibility for each other.

We can help teenagers understand how the Bible can guide them in their relationships with the opposite sex. And we can help by affirming teenagers as valuable people, worth being treated well and capable of loving with the full Christian meaning of the term.

By the end of this course your students will:
- explore positive images and motives for dating;
- gain a deeper understanding of what it means to love;
- be encouraged to make decisions based on Christian values about sexual behavior during dates; and
- discover healthy ways to deal with the painful end of romantic relationships.

COURSE OBJECTIVES

HOW TO USE THIS COURSE

ACTIVE LEARNING

Think back on an important lesson you've learned in life. Did you learn it from reading about it? from hearing about it? from something you experienced? Chances are, the most important lessons you learned came from something you experienced. That's what active learning is—learning by doing. And active learning is a key element in Group's Active Bible Curriculum.

Active learning leads students in doing things that help them understand important principles, messages and ideas. It's a discovery process that helps kids internalize what they learn.

Each lesson section in Group's Active Bible Curriculum plays an important part in active learning:

The **Opener** involves kids in the topic in fun and unusual ways.

The **Action and Reflection** includes an experience designed to evoke specific feelings in the students. This section also processes those feelings through "How did you feel?" questions and applies the message to situations kids face.

The **Bible Application** actively connects the topic with the Bible. It helps kids see how the Bible is relevant to the situations they face.

The **Commitment** helps students internalize the Bible's message and commit to make changes in their lives.

The **Closing** funnels the lesson's message into a time of creative reflection and prayer.

When you put all the sections together, you get a lesson that's fun to teach—and kids get messages they'll remember.

BEFORE THE 4-WEEK SESSION

● Read the Introduction, the Course Objectives and This Course at a Glance.

● Decide how you'll publicize the course using the art on the Publicity Page (p. 9). Prepare fliers, newsletter articles and posters as needed.

● Look at the Bonus Ideas (p. 45) and decide which ones you'll use.

● Read the opening statements, Objectives and Bible Basis for the lesson. The Bible Basis shows how specific passages relate to senior highers today.

● Choose which Opener and Closing options to use. Each is appropriate for a different kind of group. The first option is often more active.

● Gather necessary supplies from This Lesson at a Glance.

● Read each section of the lesson. Adjust where necessary for your class size and meeting room.

● The approximate minutes listed give you an idea of how long each activity will take. Each lesson is designed to take 35 to 60 minutes. Shorten or lengthen activities as needed to fit your group.

● If you see you're going to have extra time, do an activity or two from the "If You Still Have Time . . . " box or from the Bonus Ideas (p. 45).

● Dive into the activities with the kids. Don't be a spectator. The lesson will be more successful and rewarding to you and your students.

● Though some kids may at first think certain activities are "silly," they'll enjoy them, and they'll remember the messages from these activities long after the lesson is over. As one Active Bible Curriculum user has said, "I can ask the kids questions about a lesson I did three weeks ago, and they actually remember what I taught!" And that's the whole idea of teaching . . . isn't it?

Have fun with the activities you lead. Remember, it was Jesus who encouraged us to become "like little children." Besides, how often do your kids get *permission* to express their childlike qualities?

HELPFUL HINTS

● The answers given after discussion questions are responses your students *might* give. They aren't the only answers or the "right" answers. If needed, use them to spark discussion. Kids won't always say what you wish they'd say. That's why some of the responses given are negative or controversial. If someone responds negatively, don't be shocked. Accept the person, and use the opportunity to explore other angles of the issue.

THIS COURSE AT A GLANCE

Before you dive into the lessons, familiarize yourself with each lesson aim. Then read the scripture passages.
- Study them as a background to the lessons.
- Use them as a basis for your personal devotions.
- Think about how they relate to kids' circumstances today.

LESSON 1: WHY DATE?

Lesson Aim: To help senior highers form positive images and motives for dating.

Bible Basis: Luke 6:43-45 and James 1:22-25.

LESSON 2: IS IT LOVE?

Lesson Aim: To help senior highers gain a deeper understanding of what it means to love.

Bible Basis: Judges 16:4-6, 15-19, and 1 Corinthians 13:1-7.

LESSON 3: DATING AND SEX

Lesson Aim: To help senior highers base decisions about dating and sex on Christian values.

Bible Basis: 2 Samuel 11:2-5, 12-15, and Proverbs 6:27-28.

LESSON 4: BREAKING UP IS HARD TO DO

Lesson Aim: To help senior highers discover healthy ways to deal with the painful endings of romantic relationships.

Bible Basis: Colossians 3:12-14 and 1 John 4:19-21.

PUBLICITY PAGE

Grab your senior highers' attention! Copy this page, then cut and paste the art of your choice in your church bulletin or newsletter to advertise this course on dating. Or copy and use the ready-made flier as a bulletin insert. Permission to photocopy this clip art is granted for local church use.

Splash this art on posters, fliers or even postcards! Just add the vital details: the date and time the course begins, and where you'll meet. It's that simple.

Dating
Decisions

Dating
Decisions

Come to _____

On _____

At _____

Come learn what the Bible has to say about dating!

DATING DECISIONS

A 4-week high school course to help you understand what true love is

TICKETS

WHY DATE?

Dating is usually seen as a couple spending an evening together eating, playing or watching a movie. The motives for doing this can range from wanting to meet others, to a desire for romance, to a need to escape a bad home situation. We can help kids sort through their motives for dating and find creative options for dating.

To help senior highers form positive images and motives for dating.

Students will:
- **explore dating options;**
- **investigate how self-esteem affects dating;**
- **make choices about how and when to date; and**
- **see themselves as valuable and unique whether or not they date.**

Look up the following scriptures. Then read the background paragraphs to see how the passages relate to your senior highers.

In **Luke 6:43-45**, Jesus uses the image of a fig tree to describe the relationship between what we do and what's in our hearts.

Fig trees, like other fruit trees, are judged by the amount and quality of fruit they produce. Jesus says that what's in our hearts determines the kinds of actions we choose. Good actions come from a heart filled with God's goodness.

Teenagers know all about acting from their hearts. But they aren't always sure what's there. They need encouragement in forming their identities around a strong relationship with Christ so they may produce "good fruit."

James 1:22-25 reminds Christians that God's way of living is for all of life, and not just to be studied and forgotten.

James is concerned that we act on what we believe, rather than just carry our beliefs around in our heads. How we act

LESSON AIM

OBJECTIVES

BIBLE BASIS
LUKE 6:43-45
JAMES 1:22-25

says a lot about our identities . . . "like a man who looks in a mirror and sees himself as he is."

It's easy for teenagers to leave their Christian values behind once they're outside the church setting or away from Christian friends. Yet kids must learn to see these values as part of their entire lives and as a significant part of forming their identities. Dating can challenge teenagers to think about their values and identities.

THIS LESSON AT A GLANCE

Section	Minutes	What Students Will Do	Supplies
Opener (Option 1)	5 to 10	**Peanut Butter & Jelly**—Learn there's more than one way to do something.	Peanut butter, jelly, knives, bread, plastic wrap
(Option 2)		**Dating Across History**—Imagine a date in a time from the past.	
Action and Reflection	10 to 15	**Dating Grab-Bag**—Play a game and try to make trades for the "perfect" date.	"Dating Grab-Bag" cards (p. 19)
Bible Application	10 to 15	**The Invisible Date**—Learn about the importance of knowing themselves before dating.	Bibles
Commitment	10 to 15	**Bob's Big Black Book**—Complete dating profiles and make commitments about their future dating habits.	"Bob's Big Black Book" handouts (p. 20), pencils
Closing (Option 1)	up to 5	**Group Date**—Plan a group date.	
(Option 2)		**Date Faith**—Make plans to be honest about their faith in dating relationships.	Paper, pencils

The Lesson

OPENER
(5 to 10 minutes)

☐ OPTION 1: PEANUT BUTTER & JELLY

Display the ingredients for making peanut butter and jelly sandwiches so everyone can see them. Have kids each make a peanut butter and jelly sandwich. As they're working, ask questions about their different methods for making a peanut butter and jelly sandwich. For example, ask, "Why did you do this step first?" or "Other people did it this way; which is right?"

When kids are done, ask:

● **Are there different ways to make a peanut butter and jelly sandwich? Explain.** (Yes, you could do steps in a different order; yes, you can use different spreading methods.)

● **How is the variety of ways this sandwich can be made like the variety of ways you can get to know people of the opposite sex?** (You can get to know people by dating; you can get to know people by talking with them.)

Say: **Whether you've been dating for years or haven't yet been on your first date, this course can help you. Today's lesson will help you think about why and how we date and help you be more creative in how you get to know others.**

Have kids eat their sandwiches (or wrap them up for later).

☐ OPTION 2: DATING ACROSS HISTORY

Form pairs. Say: **Everyone has ideas about what to do on a date, but what would dating be like if we lived in ancient Egypt or medieval times? Take a few minutes and design a great date that might have occurred in history. You may use any historical time period you want. Be creative in your dating suggestions. For example, would ancient Egyptians take their dates to see the work being done on the Sphinx?**

After four minutes, call time and encourage the pairs to share their historical (and possibly hysterical) dates.

Say: **You did a great job of being creative in these imaginary dates, but how good do you feel about the real thing? You may've been dating for four years or may not have been on your first "real" date. Either way, this course can help you. In this lesson, we'll look at reasons people date and explore some creative ways to date.**

DATING GRAB-BAG

Explain that you're about to play a "dating" game. You'll be using cards cut apart from the "Dating Grab-Bag" handout (p. 19). Say: **The goal of this game is to design the best possible date. You'll each be given three cards and will design your date by trading cards with others until you have three that describe the "perfect date."**

To trade, just ask someone if he or she wants to make a trade. If so, both of you must hold out your cards, face down, and randomly draw one card from the other's cards. You can look at your own cards anytime, but never show others your hand. We'll play as long as people want to make trades or until I call time.

Give kids four or five minutes to trade.

After the game is finished, ask:

● **How did you feel during the game?** (Silly; unsure of what to do; like I was risking each time I traded.)

ACTION AND REFLECTION
(10 to 15 minutes)

● **What kinds of things were happening during the game?** (Some people traded a lot; some people never traded.)

● **How are the feelings or actions in this activity like the feelings or actions you experience related to dating?** (I'm usually unsure of how dates will turn out; dating is risky—just like trading the cards; you have to interact with others.)

● **Which cards did you hope to trade away?** (The ones that were boring; the stupid ones.)

● **Which cards did you hope to keep?** (The crazy and fun ones; the ones with normal dating activities.)

● **What did the game say about the way you like to date?** (It shows I like normal dates; I discovered I enjoy different kinds of dates.)

Say: **Dating means different things to different people. But the most common understanding is going out to a movie, concert or meal with a member of the opposite sex. This next activity will help us see what's important to know before we begin dating in this "one-to-one" way.**

BIBLE APPLICATION
(10 to 15 minutes)

THE INVISIBLE DATE

Have teenagers sit in chairs and form as tight a circle as possible. Say: **There's a mystery about the story I'm going to read for you. The story is called "The Invisible Date," and your job is to figure out what makes Ted disappear.**

When I've finished with my part of the story, you'll each have an opportunity to add to it. Depending on what you have Ted do, I'll tell you if Ted disappears or not. Then, based on what I tell you, you should be able to figure out what makes Ted disappear.

Read aloud "The Invisible Date" below. Then have at least three people suggest additional topics Ted discusses with his date. Use the "Understanding Ted" box (p. 15) to help you decide whether Ted disappears for each student's addition. For example, if kids suggest Ted begins talking about something personal, he wouldn't fade since the conversation shows Ted's identity. Or if kids suggest Ted begins talking about meaningless subjects, such as the weather or the latest fashion trend, he'd begin fading since the conversation doesn't help define Ted's identity.

The Invisible Date

Ted is a typical high school junior. He likes to eat, enjoys sleeping late on Saturdays, looks longingly at fast cars and requires a regular dose of sports.

Ted might seem so normal as to be uninteresting. But you haven't been on a date with him, have you?

Let's imagine your name is Tina. Because Ted considers you a prime example of why God created woman, he's asked you out on a date. You aren't sure about Ted, but decide one date won't hurt. Besides, you don't have any other plans for Friday night.

Ted shows up at your doorstep Friday night. After the usual parental inspection ritual, you both head for Ted's car.

Ted starts the car and quietly heads down Grover Street. As you glance at him to ask where you're going to eat, you're struck by the fact that Ted is looking really pale. He hasn't said more than two words since you got into the car. You ask him how he's feeling, and he snaps back: "Why? Do you think I'm sick or something? This is the way I always look. Just ask my friends." You aren't sure whether he's really upset or just trying to be funny. Just as he finishes talking, he begins to fade.

At first you think the light is playing tricks on you, but you stare at him again, and sure enough, Ted is fading away. You reach for him. But as your hand touches his shoulder, you feel the fabric of his sweater and the solid feel of his arm. Ted swerves on the road and yells: "What do you think you're doing? Do you want us to crash? What would my parents think? What would my friends think?"

You close your eyes and look again, but Ted has faded completely. There you are—alone in the car headed down the road. Just as you're about to faint, Ted starts to talk about the song that's playing on the radio.

"This is my favorite group," he begins. "I really think what they have to say is important. I'm not really into the musical style as much as the words." Suddenly Ted begins to reappear.

For the rest of the way to the restaurant, Ted tells you why he likes this group so much. You're transfixed by him. And the more Ted talks about why he likes this group, the more visible he becomes. By the time you reach the restaurant, Ted looks as normal as ever.

Inside the restaurant Ted informs you, being the man he is, he'll be getting the all-you-can-eat special. You decide to go for a salad. As you lower your menu, you gasp.

Ted's fading again. Quickly, you start a conversation with Ted, hoping to stop him from fading.

Ask volunteers to continue the story, having Ted say or do things that might make him appear or disappear. Use the hints in the "Understanding Ted" box to determine whether Ted appears or disappears.

After kids add to the story, ask:

● **Why did Ted disappear and reappear?** (He disappeared when he talked about meaningless things; he appeared when he talked about something he liked.)

After kids tell why they think Ted disappeared, read aloud the "Understanding Ted" hints.

Understanding Ted

● Ted disappears when he's putting on a front or pretending to be someone he really isn't.

● Whenever Ted begins to open up and talk about who he really is, he reappears.

● When Ted worries about what other people think of him, he fades.

Say: **Dating is designed to help us get to know one another. But if we're always pretending to be someone we're not, other people will never get to know us. We need to know who we are—and be who we are—to honestly share ourselves with others.**

Form groups of no more than five. Have groups each read aloud Luke 6:43-45; Colossians 3:8-10; and James 1:22-25.

Have groups each create a date based on these passages. Have groups decide when they'd start dating; how they'd choose who to date; where they'd go; what they'd do; and what they'd say on a date. Then have groups each tell what they designed for their date.

Ask: **How can these passages help us as we relate to members of the opposite sex?** (They remind us to be honest; they help us see the importance of being ourselves.)

Say: **When dating, it's important to be yourself, to be honest with yourself and others and to follow the guidelines outlined in the passages we read. As a Christian, your relationship with God is part of who you are, even when you're dating. Next we'll take a few minutes to discover who we are—and what we're looking for in relationships.**

COMMITMENT
(10 to 15 minutes)

BOB'S BIG BLACK BOOK

Say: **People sometimes use computerized dating services to meet other people. These services try to match people who have important similarities. Let's imagine you're using one of these services. Even though we won't be making any matches with your information, let's see how well you know yourself and what you're looking for in a date.**

Give kids each a pencil and a "Bob's Big Black Book" handout (p. 20). Have kids each complete the handout. Then form pairs and have kids briefly discuss their handouts. Have kids each say one thing they like about how their partner completed his or her handout. For example, someone might say, "I like what you said about your beliefs" or "I like the way you described your goals."

Then ask:

● **How did completing the profile make you feel? Explain.** (Uncomfortable, I didn't like what I wrote; good, I liked my profile.)

● **What did you learn about yourself by completing this handout?** (I learned that I don't know a lot about my likes and dislikes; I learned that I don't really know what I want in a dating partner.)

Give kids each a pencil and a sheet of paper. Ask them to each write three commitments about their future dating habits. For example, kids might commit to include time in future dates for discussion about faith. Or kids might commit to date for fun instead of getting serious every time.

Encourage kids to make commitments that show their desire to be honest and are in line with their Christian faith.

Say: **You're always going to be learning about yourself. But it's important to *be* yourself in relationships with others. When you're honest about who you are, you'll learn more about yourself and the people around you. And by following the scriptural guidelines, you'll grow in faith too.**

Table Talk

The Table Talk activity in this course helps senior highers talk with their parents about dating.

If you choose to use the Table Talk activity, this is a good time to show students the "Table Talk" handout (p. 21). Ask them to spend time with their parents completing it.

Before kids leave, give them each the "Table Talk" handout to take home, or tell them you'll send it to their parents.

Or use the Table Talk idea found in the Bonus Ideas (p. 46) for a meeting based on the handout.

☐ OPTION 1: GROUP DATE

Say: **One-to-one dating isn't the only way to get to know people of the opposite sex. Group dates allow you to be relaxed, be yourself and avoid the risky temptations that are often part of intimate dates.**

Help your kids plan a group date. For example, kids might choose to visit a zoo, go to a Christian concert or go out for pizza. Together, set a date for the event. After planning is completed, close in prayer asking God's presence and direction as kids make important decisions about relationships with the opposite sex.

☐ OPTION 2: DATE FAITH

Form pairs. Have partners each complete the following sentences:

● **My faith in God is important because . . .**
● **It's important to be honest about my faith in relationships because . . .**
● **I can live out my faith in dating by . . .**

Then have partners pray for each other, asking God to help them count on their faith to help them make decisions about relationships with the opposite sex.

CLOSING
(up to 5 minutes)

If You Still Have Time . . .

Talk, Talk, Talk—Have kids brainstorm subjects to talk about during a date. For example, favorite leftovers, things you like to do on Saturdays, places you used to live or your strangest dreams. Have someone list the ideas given. Then type the list and make photocopies for everyone. Suggest kids use the ideas on this list when they date.

Special Interests—Have kids design creative dates based on their interests. One at a time, ask each teenager to call out two or three favorite activities. Then have the rest of the kids help that person design dates related to those areas of interest. For example, if the interest is exercise, one dating idea might be to work out at a fitness center or gym. Or if an interest is dogs, one dating idea might be to visit the local humane society or a dog show. Remind kids to always keep their Christian values in mind when designing dates.

DATING GRAB-BAG

Make as many photocopies of this page as needed to produce three cards per teenager. Cut apart the cards and shuffle them before the session.

✂ -

Share a bologna sandwich in the rain.	Eat a picnic lunch in the park.
Enjoy dinner at a restaurant known for its great pizza.	Go shopping for a gift for a mutual friend.
Go for a ride in a horse-drawn carriage.	Spend an evening at an amusement park.
Play against each other in a racquetball game.	Take pictures of interesting people at the mall.
Go to a movie.	Play along with a prerecorded video of the morning's game shows.
Go to a friend's wedding.	Count the number of people at the mall wearing green.
Wait in line together for concert tickets .	Rate the food in children's boxed meals at fast-food restaurants.
Rent a tandem bicycle and ride to an outdoor hot-dog stand.	Draw portraits of each other using finger paints.
Spend a bunch of money at the video arcade.	Sit and stare at each other for a while.

BOB'S BIG BLACK BOOK

Date Procurement Agency
Applicant Profile
Bob's Got a Date for You!

Bob wants to know about you.

Name:	Age:	Sex:

Your interests:

Things you hate to do:

Your favorite foods:

Your least favorite foods:

Your major life goals:

Your beliefs about God:

The amount of money your date can expect you to spend on him or her:

Your good personality traits:

Your personality weaknesses:

Why you want to date:

Bob wants to know the kind of person you wish to date.

Your date's physical features:

Your date's personality traits:

Your date should care deeply about:

Your date's beliefs about God should be:

Other things you'd want to know about your date:

Table Talk

To the Parent: We're involved in a senior high course at church called *Dating Decisions*. Students are exploring a Christian perspective on dating. We'd like you and your teenager to spend some time discussing this important topic. Use this "Table Talk" page to help you do that.

Parent

Get out your old high school yearbooks and talk about the people you dated. Answer the following questions about your high school dating partners:
- Why did you date this person?
- Where did you go on dates?
- What did you do on dates?
- What do you regret about your dating activities?
- What was the best thing about your dating activities?

Senior higher

Talk with your parent about the people you'd like to date. Answer the following questions:
- Why would you like to date these people?
- Where would you like to go on dates?
- What would you like to do on dates?
- What guidelines do you think are important for your dating?

Parent and senior higher

Complete the following sentences:
- When I hear the word "dating," I think of . . .
- The most important reason for dating is . . .
- The most important reason for not dating is . . .
- The role my faith plays in dating is . . .

Talk together about dating issues, such as curfews, parties, physical affection, and appropriate and inappropriate dating activities. Come to an agreement about how you'll approach each issue.

Read Colossians 2:6-7 together and discuss it. Pray together that God will be with you in all the relationships you have with the opposite sex—in dating or in marriage.

LESSON 2

IS IT LOVE?

As they seek to know members of the opposite sex, teenagers deal with physical, psychological and social pressures. It's no surprise kids struggle to understand what it means to be in love. We can help teenagers with this struggle by letting them discover the kind of love Jesus modeled.

LESSON AIM

To help senior highers gain a deeper understanding of what it means to love.

OBJECTIVES

Students will:
- **contrast a Christian view of love with the world's view of love;**
- **understand motives for loving; and**
- **discover what it's like to feel love for someone.**

BIBLE BASIS
JUDGES 16:4-6, 15-19
1 CORINTHIANS 13:1-7

Look up the following scriptures. Then read the background paragraphs to see how the passages relate to your senior highers.

Judges 16:4-6, 15-19 contains portions of the Samson and Delilah story.

Samson was a strong Hebrew who won many battles with the Philistines. He fell in love with a Philistine woman who was paid to find the secret of his strength—his long hair. Using "If you love me" lines, she was able to betray Samson to the Philistines.

Teenagers lack experience in discerning strong feelings. They need help understanding what it means to love. And they need to learn how to identify poor motives for dating—both in themselves and others.

In **1 Corinthians 13:1-7**, Paul describes what it means to have Christ's kind of love.

The first part of this passage tells of the folly of living without love. Beginning with verse 4, Paul talks about the characteristics of God's kind of love.

Modern teenagers are bombarded from all sides with

conflicting messages about what it means to love. Television, movies and music equate love with sex, power or control. And, thanks to the messages of the "me" generation, teenagers fall into the trap of caring more about being loved than about loving others. When they date, teenagers need to have a knowledge of and commitment to Christ's kind of love.

THIS LESSON AT A GLANCE

Section	Minutes	What Students Will Do	Supplies
Opener (Option 1)	up to 5	**I Love . . .**—Play a guessing game about things people love.	
(Option 2)		**Love, TV Style**—Identify different ideas of love from popular TV shows.	Paper, pencils
Action and Reflection	10 to 15	**Love Sleuth**—Act as detectives searching for evidence of people's love for each other.	"How Do You Know What Love Is?" handouts (p. 28), newsprint, marker
Bible Application	10 to 15	**Locks of Love**—Design advertisements for a movie based on the story of Samson and Delilah.	Bibles, posterboard, markers
Commitment	10 to 15	**If You Love Me . . .**—Decide what loving means.	"If You Love Me . . ." handouts (p. 29), pencils, Bibles
Closing (Option 1)	5 to 10	**The Lovables**—Identify things about each other that make them lovable.	3×5 cards, pencils
(Option 2)		**Lovin' Spoonfuls**—Experience the joy of sharing love.	Spoons, honey

The Lesson

☐ OPTION 1: I LOVE ...

Play this game much like I Spy. But instead of saying, "I spy something . . . ," have kids say, "I love something . . ." and then give a partial description of the item. For example, kids might say, "I love something you have to plug in" (a radio) or "I love something sweet" (chocolate cake). Have teenagers take turns beginning "I love something . . ." statements while the rest of the kids try to guess what they're thinking of. Kids may ask up to 10 yes or no questions to discover what the person is thinking of.

When kids have each had a turn to think of something,

OPENER
(up to 5 minutes)

say: **We use the word "love" to talk about a lot of things. We say we love chocolate, sports cars and water-skiing. But when we speak about loving people, we aren't always as sure what we're talking about. In this session, we'll work together to better understand what it means to love someone.**

☐ OPTION 2: LOVE, TV STYLE

Form groups of no more than three. Give groups each a sheet of paper and a pencil. Say: **On your paper, list two TV shows that portray love in some way. Then, for each show, write what the show's definition of love might be.**

Allow three minutes for kids to brainstorm ideas. Then have groups each tell what they wrote.

Say: **There are many different ideas about what it means to love—especially on television. As you date, how do you know whether your upset stomach means you're in love or that you had too much pizza? In this session, we'll take a look at what it means to love according to God's definition.**

Table Talk Follow-Up

If you sent the "Table Talk" handout (p. 21) to parents last week, discuss students' reactions to the activity. Ask volunteers to share what they learned from the discussion with their parents.

ACTION AND REFLECTION

(10 to 15 minutes)

LOVE SLEUTH

Say: **When you get to know someone by spending time together, you may start to feel hard-to-describe feelings about that person. You may wonder, "Is this love?" Today we'll explore what love is and how you can know whether you're in love with someone.**

Give kids each a section from the "How Do You Know What Love Is?" handout (p. 28). It's okay to have more than one person with the same section. Tell kids to not reveal to anyone what their sections say.

Say: **In a moment, I'll ask you to follow the instructions on your handout. Your job is to find other people who have the same instructions you do. You may not tell anyone what your handout says or show it to anyone. You must try to figure out who else has the same instructions based on the way they act or talk.**

Allow teenagers a minute to read their instructions. Then have kids mingle and talk among themselves according to their instructions. After five minutes, call time.

Ask:

● **How easy was it to find others with the same**

instructions? Explain. (Not very easy, people were doing different things; somewhat easy, I could identify similar things someone else was doing.)

● **How did you feel as you tried to find others with the same instructions?** (Uncomfortable; nervous; silly.)

● **How is trying to find others with the same instructions like trying to understand what love is?** (It's not easy; sometimes you think you know what it is but find out you're wrong.)

● **What do each of the instruction sections say about love?** (Love is giving of yourself; love is getting what you can from someone; love is sometimes boastful; physical beauty is important in relationships; faith is important in love relationships.)

● **What are ways people define love?** List on newsprint the ideas kids call out.

● **Based on this activity and the ideas listed on the newsprint, what can we conclude about what love is?** (Love means different things to different people; love is difficult to define; love means caring for others.)

Say: **Love is often given or received for different reasons. Next we're going to look at how motives can help us know what's true love and what isn't. And we'll explore what the Bible says about love.**

LOCKS OF LOVE

Form groups of no more than six and give each group a Bible. Have groups each read Judges 16:4-6, 15-19. Give groups each a sheet of posterboard and markers.

Say: **Use your posterboard to create an advertisement for the story of Samson and Delilah as it might be told in a modern movie. For example, you might make Samson a wealthy businessman and Delilah a sly secretary of a rival business who plots to topple Samson's successful business. On your posters, list the basic plot of your story and illustrate it.**

After seven minutes, have groups each present their movie advertisement.

Then ask:

● **How would you describe Samson's and Delilah's motives for being together?** (Samson had a romantic love for Delilah; Delilah cared for Samson only because of what he could do for her.)

● **How can motives for dating affect a relationship?** (If the motives are different, it can cause trouble; if one person is serious about the date, but the other just wants to have fun, feelings can get hurt.)

Read aloud 1 Corinthians 13:1-7.

Ask:

● **How is Christian love different from the world's idea of love?** (God's love isn't proud; God's love doesn't keep a record of wrongs; God's love means never giving up on someone; God's love lasts forever.)

Say: **According to this passage in 1 Corinthians, love isn't selfish. When you get to know someone through dating, you may begin to wonder what draws you together. One way to test your love for each other is to examine how well you follow the ideas in 1 Corinthians 13:1-7.**

IF YOU LOVE ME . . .

Give kids each a Bible, a pencil and an "If You Love Me . . ." handout (p. 29). Have kids each reread 1 Corinthians 13:1-7 and complete the handout.

Then form groups of no more than four. Have kids sit in circles and talk about their completed handouts in their groups. Have kids each choose one or two "If you love me . . ." statements they'll work on in their lives during the coming weeks. Also, have them briefly discuss the questions at the bottom of the page.

After a couple of minutes, say: **God not only commands us to love, but shows us a way of loving that brings out the best in ourselves and others. If we keep our love for God at the center of our hearts, we'll make good decisions about how to love others.**

 **OPTION 1: THE LOVABLES**

Have kids sit in a circle. Give kids each a pencil and enough 3×5 cards to be able to write a note to each class member. If your group is larger than 10, form circles of no more than 10. Give kids each enough cards to be able to write notes to everyone in their circle.

Say: **Each of us has unique characteristics that make us lovable. Without signing your cards, write a positive "you're lovable" statement to everyone else in your circle. For example, you might write, "You're lovable because you're easygoing" or "You're lovable because you're patient."**

When you've finished, place each card on the floor behind the chair of the person it's for.

Allow a few minutes for kids to write on their cards and distribute them. Then close in prayer, thanking God for giving us the ability to show love to one another like he wants us to.

Have kids read their cards and take them home as reminders of their lovability.

OPTION 2: LOVIN' SPOONFULS

Have kids stand in a circle. Give kids each a spoon. Say: **Christian love should be something sweet we give to one another. To symbolize this, I want you to feed the person on your left whatever I place on your spoon. As you do**

COMMITMENT
(10 to 15 minutes)

CLOSING
(5 to 10 minutes)

this, tell that person something you appreciate about him or her. Remember we're all capable of giving and receiving love.

Go around the circle and place a few drops of honey on each spoon. It's okay if kids laugh or giggle with this activity. If they seem uncomfortable "feeding" each other, ask kids why they feel that way. Help kids see how God's love sometimes can be uncomfortable. Remind kids that the honey represents the kind of love God wants them to show to each other—in dating and in other relationships.

Have volunteers close in prayer, asking God for guidance in dating relationships.

If You Still Have Time ...

Thanks for the Lovin'—Have kids each write a thank-you note to someone in the church who's shown love to them. Encourage kids to think of people who exemplify the love outlined in 1 Corinthians 13:1-7. Then have kids deliver the "love notes" to the appropriate people.

Radio Love—Form groups of no more than four. Have groups discuss popular songs about love. Have kids explore what the songs really say about love and compare those definitions of love with the love outlined in 1 Corinthians 13:1-7.

HOW DO YOU KNOW WHAT LOVE IS?

Photocopy and cut apart the following sections and distribute one to each teenager.

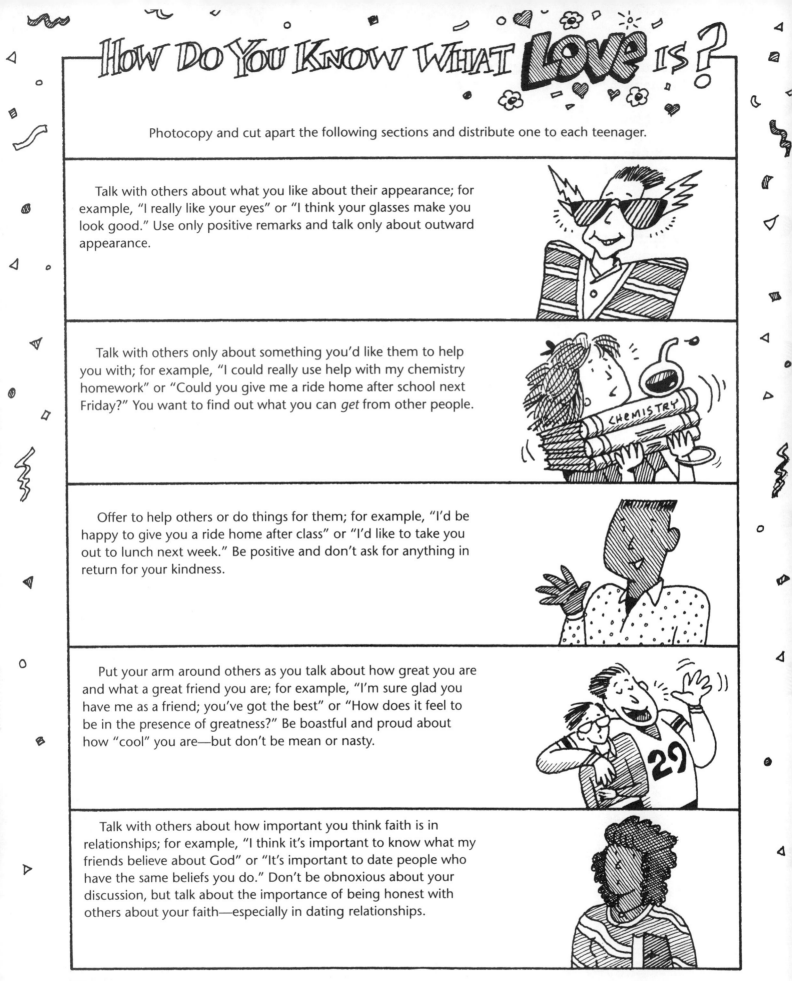

Talk with others about what you like about their appearance; for example, "I really like your eyes" or "I think your glasses make you look good." Use only positive remarks and talk only about outward appearance.

Talk with others only about something you'd like them to help you with; for example, "I could really use help with my chemistry homework" or "Could you give me a ride home after school next Friday?" You want to find out what you can *get* from other people.

Offer to help others or do things for them; for example, "I'd be happy to give you a ride home after class" or "I'd like to take you out to lunch next week." Be positive and don't ask for anything in return for your kindness.

Put your arm around others as you talk about how great you are and what a great friend you are; for example, "I'm sure glad you have me as a friend; you've got the best" or "How does it feel to be in the presence of greatness?" Be boastful and proud about how "cool" you are—but don't be mean or nasty.

Talk with others about how important you think faith is in relationships; for example, "I think it's important to know what my friends believe about God" or "It's important to date people who have the same beliefs you do." Don't be obnoxious about your discussion, but talk about the importance of being honest with others about your faith—especially in dating relationships.

IF YOU LOVE ME...

"If you love me, you'll . . ." is a line we sometimes hear from people we care about.

But these requests aren't loving at all. In fact, they're selfish and manipulative. But we can turn these negative statements into challenges to love according to God's definition of love.

Read 1 Corinthians 13:1-7. Use the comments on love found there to complete the following "If you love me" statements as if you were saying them to people you'd like to date. For example: If you love me, you'll be patient with me and not rush me into things I don't want.

Add your positive "If you love me" statements below:

- If you love me, you'll . . .

- If you love me, you'll . . .

- If you love me, you'll . . .

- If you love me, you'll . . .

- If you love me, you'll . . .

Discussion Questions

- Have you ever been manipulated by someone's "If you love me" statements? If so, how did knowing you'd been "used" make you feel?
- How important are people's motives for developing love relationships? Explain.
- What does it mean to love someone unselfishly?
- Is it easy to love others unselfishly? Why or why not?

LESSON 3

DATING AND SEX

Teenagers are looking for ways to date that are fun and exciting. But thanks to peer pressure, teenagers are forced into thinking that dating usually leads to sexual involvement. We can help teenagers see there are many fun dating alternatives that don't carry the risks, responsibilities and hurts of sexual involvement.

LESSON AIM

To help senior highers base decisions about dating and sex on Christian values.

OBJECTIVES

Students will:
- discover the connection between sexual behaviors and consequences;
- see how their choices about physical relationships affect others; and
- determine their limits in resisting sexual temptation.

BIBLE BASIS

2 SAMUEL 11:2-5, 12-15
PROVERBS 6:27-28

Look up the following scriptures. Then read the background paragraphs to see how the passages relate to your senior highers.

Second Samuel 11:2-5, 12-15 describes the story of David and Bathsheba.

David was a popular and successful king. This story of David's desire—and the consequences of his actions—shows the great power of sexual feelings and the effect these feelings can have when they're out of control.

Teenagers enjoy the freedoms of thinking and decision-making, but lack the experience to always see the consequences of their actions. Like David, a teenager may enter into a sexual act thinking it's his or her decision only and that the consequences won't affect anyone else. Kids need to see that their sexual activities affect the lives of many other people (partners, parents, friends, future spouses, possible children) and God.

Proverbs 6:27-28 discusses the inevitable consequences of our actions.

The wise writer of Proverbs uses two "hot" images to show the connection between actions and consequences. Carrying a fire against your chest will burn your clothes, and walking on hot coals will burn your feet. Likewise, committing a sexual sin will bring painful results.

With movies and television showing the pleasure of sex (and often avoiding the negative consequences), teenagers can easily be misled into wrong sexual decisions. And although kids know of the dangers of sexual involvement, their "It won't happen to me" attitudes give them a false sense of security in their decisions to have sex. Kids need to be reminded that sexual relations require the responsible commitment found in marriage. If walking on hot coals will burn a person's feet, mixing sex and dating will burn a teenager's heart!

THIS LESSON AT A GLANCE

Section	Minutes	What Students Will Do	Supplies
Opener (Option 1)	5 to 10	**Fantastic Fantasy**—Imagine a situation they'd really enjoy.	
(Option 2)		**Kissing Contest**—View and rate kisses as seen on TV shows and commercials.	Television, VCR, video-cassette, 3×5 cards, pencils
Action and Reflection	10 to 15	**Weighty Choices**—Try to win a "heavy" guessing game.	Paper bags, sealable plastic bags, scale, water, food prize, paper, pencil
Bible Application	10 to 15	**Love Connection**—Experience how their actions affect others.	Ball of yarn, Bibles
Commitment	5 to 10	**Dating Steam-Meter**—Discover when they feel out of control in tempting sexual situations.	"Dating Steam-Meter" handouts (p. 37), pencils
Closing (Option 1)	5 to 10	**Defensive Maneuvers**—Find creative ways to avoid tempting situations.	Paper, pencils
(Option 2)		**101 Ideas**—Brainstorm dating activities that avoid opportunities for sexual temptation.	Paper, pencils

The Lesson

☐ OPTION 1: FANTASTIC FANTASY

Say: **Have you ever dreamed of going somewhere really fun, or doing something outrageous, or owning something incredibly expensive? Well, if you haven't thought about any of these things recently, here's your big chance. For the next few minutes, I want you to think quietly about any of these things: a place you'd like to visit, an adventure you'd like to experience or a purchase you'd love to make. In a few minutes, we'll talk about your ideas.**

Remind kids to be quiet during this time. You might want to play quiet music while kids think about what they'd do.

After a few minutes, ask:

● **How did you feel as you thought about your fantasy?** (Carefree; like nothing could go wrong; hopeful.)

Say: **Now think about the negative aspects of your fantasy. What could go wrong or be harmful in what you were thinking about?**

Allow a couple of minutes for kids to think about the negative sides of their fantasies.

Ask:

● **What surprised you about the negative sides of your fantasies?** (I didn't think there would be negatives; there were a lot of negatives.)

● **How is that like sexual involvement in dating?** (There are lots of hidden negatives; sexual involvement has serious consequences.)

Say: **As you may've discovered, fantasies are great until we think about the negative consequences or responsibilities that come with them. In dating, the prospect of a sexual relationship outside of marriage can also seem wonderful—until we realize the potential negative consequences it could bring. Today we'll discover how our Christian faith can help us deal with the issue of sex in dating.**

☐ OPTION 2: KISSING CONTEST

Before the session, videotape five to eight brief excerpts of people kissing on TV shows or commercials. Set up a VCR and television and be prepared to show the clips during class. A few good places to find people kissing are on soap operas, prime-time dramas and TV movies.

When kids arrive, say: **We're going to start today's lesson by having a kissing contest!** (Pause to allow kids to groan or cheer.) **Before you pucker up, let me point out that the kisses we'll be comparing are all on this videocassette.**

As you watch the video kisses, rate each on a scale of 1 to 10, with 10 being the best.

Give kids each a 3×5 card and a pencil. Have kids each number along the side of their card from 1 to 8 (or however many kisses you've recorded). Play the video and call out the number of the kiss they're rating as it's being shown. You might want to show the video two or three times. When the contest is over, tally the results to determine the winning kiss.

Ask:

● **What made this kiss the winner?** (It was the longest kiss; it was the sexiest kiss; the people seemed to enjoy it most.)

● **How did you feel choosing the best kiss?** (Uncomfortable; silly; awkward.)

● **How is that like the way people feel as they get closer physically?** (They feel awkward; they feel uncomfortable.)

Say: **Kissing is a common component of dating. But if you aren't careful, something as simple as kissing can lead to more risky behavior. In this lesson we'll look at sex and dating—and learn how our faith can help us make healthy decisions about both.**

WEIGHTY CHOICES

Place varying amounts of water in sealable plastic bags. Make sure the partially empty bags are inflated with air so they'll take up the same space as those filled with water.

Place plastic bags each in a separate paper bag so kids can't tell how much the paper bags weigh by looking at them. Be sure to have at least 10 bags for this activity. Line up the bags on a table. Have a scale available that can measure as little as 2 pounds.

Show teenagers the bags and the scale. Say: **In a moment, you'll compete to see who can identify how many bags it takes to weigh 2 pounds. The person who's closest to 2 pounds without going over will win a prize.**

Here's how it works: When it's your turn to guess, you must choose which bags you'll place on the scale. Once you touch a bag, you must use it. You may only place the bags on the scale once you've chosen all you're going to use.

Beginning with the person who got up the earliest this morning, have kids each take a turn choosing bags and placing them on the scale. Warn kids not to be too rough with the bags. As kids each choose which bags they want, encourage them to "take just one more." Tell kids how disappointed you feel when they go over the 2-pound limit.

Put the bags back on the table after each person is done and record the weight on a sheet of paper. Give the person who comes closest to 2 pounds a food prize, such as a bag of cookies.

Then ask:
- **How did you feel during the game?** (Competitive, I wanted to win; scared I'd mess up; cautious; adventurous.)
- **What was your strategy?** (To find the heavy bags; to get only a certain number of bags.)
- **How tempting was it to take "just one more"? Explain.** (Very, because we wanted to look like we knew what we were doing; not very, with my luck I'd choose the wrong weight.)
- **How is the temptation to take "one more bag" like the temptation to explore sex in dating?** (You think you know what you're doing but it can turn out differently; you're tempted to go just a little further each time; you can go past your limit without really meaning to.)
- **Why do people who are dating feel pressure to explore sexual feelings?** (Because friends tell them having sex is "cool"; because they feel attracted to each other physically; because they think it's normal to develop a physical relationship.)

Say: **When two people begin serious dating, they become closer in many ways. And the pressure to give in to sexual desires becomes stronger and stronger. Unfortunately, dealing with these desires isn't always easy. And sometimes people make decisions they later regret. Thankfully, the Bible offers helpful advice about how to deal with the issue of sex and dating.**

BIBLE APPLICATION
(10 to 15 minutes)

LOVE CONNECTION

Have volunteers read aloud 2 Samuel 11:2-5, 12-15. Then say: **When we make choices, we must be ready for the consequences. But the consequences don't only affect the people making the decisions. David and Bathsheba may've been ready to deal with the choices they made, but what about Uriah, who eventually died because of their choices? Part of making good decisions about dating and sex is to remember that your actions affect other people.**

Have teenagers stand in a circle. Place a ball of yarn in the center of the circle. Weave the yarn in between and around the teenagers to "tie them up" as you read aloud the following sentences. Pause as necessary to allow enough time to completely entangle the kids during your talk.

Say: **You're on a date and things start getting physical. You know having sex before marriage is risky, but you think, "Hey, it's my life and my decision." Yet before you act on this thought, the faces of people you know start forming in your mind. And in your heart, lines are drawn to ...**
- **... people who trust your judgment;**
- **... people you love and who love you;**
- **... your parents;**
- **... your grandparents;**

... **your Christian friends;**
... **your favorite teacher;**
... **your youth leaders at church;**
... **your future husband or wife;**
... **Jesus.**

When teenagers are connected in several directions, say: **Look at the love lines connecting us, and think about all the ways we connect with people outside this room. Sex is a deeply personal gift; it changes us when we share it. And when we change, it affects all the other relationships in our lives. If people spread rumors, a partner feels used, a pregnancy occurs or a disease is spread, others are even more deeply affected.**

● **How did you feel about being connected with the yarn?** (Uncomfortable; nervous; unsure.)

● **How is this like the way people feel when they consider the consequences of sexual involvement?** (They feel uncomfortable; they feel nervous.)

Read aloud Proverbs 6:27-28.

Ask:

● **How does this passage apply to dating and sex?** (If you play around sexually, you'll have to face the consequences.)

The next time you're tempted to give in to sexual desires on a date, remember that you're "all tied up" in lines of love—and that the consequences you might face affect more than just two people.

Have kids untangle themselves and return to their seats.

DATING STEAM-METER

Give kids each a pencil and a "Dating Steam-Meter" handout (p. 37). Say: **Use this handout to help you think about where you begin to feel "out of control" in a physical relationship. You won't need to show this to anyone. When you're done, read and sign the commitment at the bottom of the page. Then find a partner and encourage him or her to act responsibly on dates; for example, say, "God will keep you strong when you're tempted" or "You can overcome the temptation to go too far." Take a moment to pray with your partner for wisdom in your dating decisions.**

☐ OPTION 1: DEFENSIVE MANEUVERS

Say: **Have you ever wondered how to gracefully get out of a sticky or overly tempting situation? Let's work together to find creative ways out of awkward situations.**

Form groups of no more than three, and give each group a sheet of paper and a pencil. Have groups each brainstorm at least four situations where a dating partner is being tempted sexually. Then have groups each describe their suggestions and act one out for the whole group. Have kids brainstorm

COMMITMENT
(5 to 10 minutes)

CLOSING
(5 to 10 minutes)

creative ways to get out of each situation; for example, "If a group describes a situation where a dating partner wants to kiss you, say you don't want to spread germs."

Close by having kids pass the yarn from Love Connection around a circle as they take turns praying for good judgment in decisions regarding sex and dating.

☐ OPTION 2: 101 IDEAS

Say: **The key to avoiding tempting sexual situations is to avoid dates that would easily lend themselves to "getting physical," such as going to a romantic movie or watching television together in an otherwise empty house.**

Form groups of no more than five. Give groups each a sheet of paper and a pencil. Have groups each list dating activities that avoid opportunities for sexual involvement.

After a couple of minutes, have groups each tell what they brainstormed. Ask kids to commit to dating activities such as those listed and to stay away from activities that will tempt them sexually. Have volunteers close in prayer, asking God's guidance in issues of sex and dating.

If You Still Have Time . . .

Private Conversations—Give kids each a sheet of paper and a pencil. Have them each write questions they have about sex and dating. Tell kids you'll discuss the questions with a pastor or other church professional and report your discoveries in class next week. Assure kids their questions will remain anonymous. Encourage kids to ask questions about appropriate sexual behaviors as they relate to faith.

Teasers Beware!—Form two groups—one of all guys and the other of all girls. Have groups each discuss how guys and girls sexually "tease" each other by the way they dress, talk or act. Have groups talk about how this teasing does or doesn't fit with Christian faith. Then have groups report their discoveries back to the whole group.

The closer you get to someone physically, the more tempted you are to "go further." And when you're in the "heat of the moment," it's never easy to set limits on your physical relationship. Many times, people let their hormones guide them into sexual involvement, only to later feel regret or guilt for their hasty actions.

On the meter below, mark what your physical limits will be. Your mark should be below the level where you'd feel "out of control" if you went that far. Be honest. No one will see your answers. Then, seriously evaluate your physical limits by completing the questions below.

Answer the following questions:
- Is it easy to limit the physical aspect of a dating relationship? Why or why not?
- What is an appropriate limit for sexual activity in dating?
- How would God feel about the limit you've chosen on the Dating Steam-Meter?
- Why does God want us to wait until the commitment of marriage to experience sexual fulfillment?

Complete the following sentences:
- I date (or want to date) because:
- One thing I'll do to avoid sexual temptation in dating is:
- When I look at my mark on the Dating Steam-Meter, I feel:

Commitment:
I commit to follow God's will in my dating. I'll talk with Christian friends and teachers when I have doubts about what's okay or not okay in my love relationships. I'll seek guidance on proper limits of physical expression. And if I've already made sexual mistakes, I'll ask God to help me.

Signature:_____

LESSON 4

BREAKING UP IS HARD TO DO

Teenagers often enter serious romantic relationships during high school. The intensity of feelings involved and inexperience in relating make painful breakups a common event. Teenagers need to learn skills to help them end relationships in healthy ways. We can help teenagers learn these skills—and help them discover where to find comfort after the painful breakups they'll likely encounter.

LESSON AIM

To help senior highers discover healthy ways to deal with the painful endings of romantic relationships.

OBJECTIVES

Students will:
- **explore feelings related to breaking up;**
- **experience and reflect on the harshness of breakups;**
- **discover positive ways to deal with broken relationships; and**
- **ask God to help them deal with painful times.**

BIBLE BASIS

COLOSSIANS 3:12-14
1 JOHN 4:19-21

Look up the following scriptures. Then read the background paragraphs to see how the passages relate to your senior highers.

In **Colossians 3:12-14**, Paul tells members of the Colossian church how Christians should relate with each other.

In this passage, Paul explains how we're made new creations in Christ and how being new creations changes who we are and how we should act.

When a romance ends, it's easy to focus on the hurt and anger and to become hateful or bitter. While breakups are almost always painful, learning to take Paul's advice on how to treat others can ease the pain teenagers feel.

In **1 John 4:19-21**, John writes about how our love for God leads us to relate appropriately with others.

It's impossible to love God and hate others. Instead, our love of God should lead us to also treat others with respect and care.

Revenge is a common response to the pain of breakups. Since broken romances often end in disagreement or wrong-doing, teenagers sometimes turn the affection they once felt for another into hate. Teenagers need to discover positive ways to respond to the anger and loss of broken relationships. The love of God is available to comfort and heal their pain.

THIS LESSON AT A GLANCE

Section	Minutes	What Students Will Do	Supplies
Opener (Option 1)	5 to 10	**Sticky Business**—Try to separate two substances without hurting either one.	Cellophane tape, construction paper
(Option 2)		**Fond Memories**—Remember feelings from past relationships.	
Action and Reflection	15 to 20	**Knot in Love**—Make strong knots in yarn and see what happens when they try to quickly untie them.	Balls of yarn, scissors
Bible Application	10 to 15	**Graceful Parting**—Discover strategies for parting ways, based on Bible passages.	"Graceful Parting" handouts (p. 44), pencils, Bibles
Commitment	5 to 10	**Heart Patches**—Make a symbolic heart-patching first-aid kit.	Tape, paper, markers
Closing (Option 1)	up to 5	**The Bandage Pact**—Apply bandages to each other as symbols of support.	Adhesive bandages
(Option 2)		**Celebration of Survival**—Brainstorm ways people can become "survivors" of broken relationships.	

The Lesson

☐ OPTION 1: STICKY BUSINESS

Before the session, place several pieces of cellophane tape on a sheet of construction paper and press them down so no edges of the tape can be easily lifted.

OPENER
(5 to 10 minutes)

Have volunteers each try to remove a piece of tape without taking any of the construction paper with it.

Then ask:

● **How is trying to separate the tape cleanly from the construction paper like trying to make a "clean break" in a dating relationship?** (It isn't easy; breaking up is often painful and leaves scars on both people.)

Then say: **Just as the tape was attached securely to this paper, you may be closely attached to another person in a romantic relationship. And just as the paper was torn when we tried to pull off the tape, you may feel torn up when your relationship ends. Today we'll discover ways to handle a broken romantic relationship.**

☐ OPTION 2: FOND MEMORIES

Ask teenagers to each remember a favorite friend, relative, boyfriend or girlfriend from their past. Tell kids to think of someone they no longer have a close relationship with.

Say: **Picture in your mind the face of the person from your past.** (pause) **Think of things that person would say.** (pause) **Picture yourself doing something with the other person. Remember the good times.** (pause)

Ask:

● **How did you feel as you imagined this person?** (Warm; sad; indifferent; angry.)

● **Did the way the relationship ended affect the way you were able to remember the good times?** (Yes, I could only think of how my friend hurt me; no, I still treasure the fun times.)

Say: **Sometimes the passage of time helps us look at old relationships in a new way. Today's session will help us learn how to handle painful breakups in our romantic relationships and find ways to remember more than just the bad times.**

ACTION AND REFLECTION
(15 to 20 minutes)

KNOT IN LOVE

Before the lesson, cut several 4-foot lengths of two different colors of yarn. Cut enough so each person can have one strand.

Form two groups. Give kids in one group each one strand of the same-color yarn. Give kids in the other group each one strand of the other color yarn.

Say: **For the first part of this activity, you must connect your strand of yarn to at least one strand of the other color yarn. Each strand can be tied to more than one strand of the other color, so make all the knots you want! The only rule is you must keep track of your yarn strand—so don't let go of it once you've tied it to other yarn strands. Now, see how well you can connect this yarn and let's make those knots secure!**

When kids have tied many knots, say: **For the second part of this activity, you must separate your strand from every other strand it's connected to. You'll only have one minute to do this. If you want to use scissors, you may. But when time is up, all strands must be separated.**

Provide scissors for kids who want them. After one minute, call time. Have kids each toss their yarn in the middle of the floor and sit down.

Ask:

● **What were your feelings while tying the strands together?** (I enjoyed it; it was challenging.)

● **How did you feel when I told you they had to come apart?** (I was disappointed; I felt rushed; I was confused.)

● **How did the time limit to separate the strands affect your work?** (We couldn't untie all the knots and had to cut some of them; we couldn't do the job we wanted.)

● **How is the way we tied yarn together like the way romantic relationships develop?** (People spend a lot of time together; people get close to each other in many ways.)

● **How are the feelings we had when we rushed to untie all the knots like the feelings we have when romantic relationships end?** (We feel unprepared for the separation; we feel hurt or confused; we feel angry or upset.)

Say: **If you could predict your future in relationships, you could avoid all relationships that would eventually break up. Yet, since you can't predict your future, most of you will probably feel the agony of separation in a dating relationship sometime in your life. And when two people break up, they often feel angry or spiteful toward each other. Let's see what the Bible says about handling these painful times.**

GRACEFUL PARTING

Give kids each a Bible, a pencil and a "Graceful Parting" handout (p. 44). Say: **It's easy to get angry and bitter when a breakup occurs, but God knows how damaging such feelings and behaviors are to others and ourselves. See if you can help the couple described here find good ideas on how to break up less painfully.**

Allow four minutes for kids to complete their handouts. Then have kids each find a partner and discuss the questions at the bottom of their handout.

After a few minutes, form a circle. Have kids tell what they learned in their discussions.

Ask:

● **What can we learn from the scriptures that will help in dealing with painful breakups?** (Be patient with others; show love even to people you don't like; be kind to the person you're breaking up with.)

Say: **Breaking up can be one of the most painful experiences you'll ever have. That's why it's important to ask** for God's help when you're in the middle of a breakup and as you deal with the lasting pain.

HEART PATCHES

Form groups of no more than four. In the middle of the room, place paper, tape and markers. Say: **When we get cuts and scrapes on our bodies, we usually reach for a first-aid kit to stop the pain and help the healing. Use the materials provided to make a breaking-up first-aid kit. As you design your medical supplies, label them to reflect the "symptoms" they address. For example, you might make an ointment called HeartCream that soothes the pain of loss.**

Encourage kids to incorporate the advice from scripture in their kits. Give groups about seven minutes; then form a circle and have groups each explain what they included in their breaking-up first-aid kit. After groups have shown their kits, have kids each say what they like most about another group's kit. For example, someone might say, "I really like the way they included encouragement in their kit" or "I really like the creative way they made their supplies."

Say: **The ideas you presented in your first-aid kits can help you deal with the difficult experiences of broken relationships. And God can help us grow beyond the pain we feel. Take a moment to silently ask for God's help in dealing with breaking up.**

☐ OPTION 1: THE BANDAGE PACT

Give kids each three adhesive bandages. Say: **These bandages symbolize our ability to help each other find comfort in painful times such as breakups. One way we can help is by encouraging each other. Go around to three other people and place a bandage on each of them. As you do, say something you appreciate about that person. For example, you might say, "I appreciate your kindness" or "I'm impressed by your patience."**

If your kids like to sing, consider singing "Lean on Me," "You've Got a Friend" or a similar song your kids know. Have a volunteer close in prayer, asking God for love, forgiveness and humility in our relationships with others.

☐ OPTION 2: CELEBRATION OF SURVIVAL

Say: **We've all seen how injured athletes have often come back stronger after they've recovered from their injuries. In a similar way, living through the pain of a broken relationship can help us "come back stronger" in our relationships with others.**

Ask:

● **Have you ever had a difficult breakup? If so, what did**

you learn from that experience that can help you in the future? (Yes, I learned not to base a relationship on outward appearance; yes, I learned not to get too serious in relation-ships.)

If kids haven't experienced breakups, tell of experiences in your life that resulted in broken relationships.

After a few volunteers discuss what they've learned, have the group applaud the "survivors" of broken relationships. Have volunteers close in prayer, asking God to help them look to him for healing and for strength to be survivors in painful times.

If You Still Have Time . . .

Risky Business—Ask kids to list and debate risks involved in serious dating. Help them see that the more they reveal about themselves—emotionally, spiritually, physically—the more painful the breakup is likely to be.

Course Reflection—Form a circle. Ask students to reflect on the past four lessons. Have them take turns completing the following sentences:
- Something I learned in this course was . . .
- If I could tell my friends about this course, I'd say . . .
- Something I'll do differently because of this course is . . .

Graceful PARTING

Read the following scenario. Then look up and read the scripture passages listed. Use the advice from the Bible and your own common sense to suggest ways for Vince and Sally to part gracefully following the end of their romance.

Vince and Sally had been going steady for six months. When Sally saw Vince out with Carla, she decided it was time to end the relationship. Here are the reasons each gave for the breakup:

Sally: If Vince hadn't always counted on me to plan things for our dates, we'd still be together. But he expected me to do all the work in our relationship. How can someone be so ungrateful? And that thing with Carla . . . well, I don't think it's the first time Vince has gone out behind my back. Who needs him?

Vince: It was Sally's fault. She was suffocating me and trying to get too serious. I had to do something to get out. Besides, I was just going out with Carla as a friend. Can't I have friends of the opposite sex? I can't believe how blind Sally's been! Who needs her?

Vince and Sally aren't talking to each other. Both are angry at each other and the way the relationship ended. Use the following scriptures to come up with ways they could handle the breakup better: Colossians 3:12-14 and 1 John 4:19-21. Use the space below to list your ideas.

Discussion Questions:
- Why do relationships often end painfully?
  - What can you do in romantic relationships to minimize the pain of a breakup?
    - How can the traits described in Colossians 3:12-14 help you deal with a broken relationship?
      - How can your faith help you deal with a broken relationship?
        - Is it possible to remain friends with someone you used to date? Why or why not?

BONUS IDEAS

Great Dates—Have kids brainstorm dates they'd go on if they had unlimited resources. List these ideas on newsprint. Then have kids brainstorm dates they'd go on if they had no money to spend. List these on a separate sheet of newsprint. Have kids discuss what makes a dating experience worthwhile. Get a copy of the book *Creative Dating* by Doug Fields and Todd Temple (Oliver-Nelson) to spark ideas for creative and inexpensive dates.

Dating Videos—Interview kids in front of a video camera as if they were signing up with a dating service. Ask teenagers questions about themselves, what they care about and how they stand on dating issues such as sex or going steady. Formulate the questions so kids will think about what's important to them; for example, "What's most important to you in relationships with others?" "What things interest you most?" or "What things bother you most?"

If kids are willing, play the videotapes for the whole group and discuss what people learned from the videos about each other and themselves. Give kids their videotapes to take home as a reminder of "who they are" and what they think is important in dating.

Just Call Me—Form groups of no more than four and have them each create a funny or serious skit about dating that somehow uses a telephone as a prop. Encourage kids to be creative in how they use the telephone in their skits.

Have groups each perform their skit for the whole group. Encourage discussion about each skit, and have kids tell what they thought was realistic or unrealistic.

Out of the Hot Seat—Have kids brainstorm specific ways to avoid or get out of tempting sexual situations while dating. Have kids come up with things to say or do to help them avoid getting physically intimate during a date. For fun, have kids role play a few of the ideas. Have guys play the girls' roles and girls play the guys' roles.

The Dating Box—Set up a box for kids to drop in creative dating ideas and methods for asking someone out on a date. Award a prize for the most creative dating idea. Collect the ideas and publish them in a newsletter. Add scriptural advice applicable to dating and mail a copy to each teenager.

MEETINGS AND MORE

Dating Survey—Help kids develop a dating survey that includes questions such as "How important is the physical relationship in dating?" "How does what you believe about God affect your dating relationships?" or "How important is open communication in dating?" Then have kids get permission to distribute the survey at school. Also, have kids interview senior citizens about their dating experiences. Plan a meeting to discuss the completed handouts. Use comments on the surveys to spark discussion about dating issues.

Table Talk—Use the "Table Talk" handout (p. 21) as the basis for a parents and teenagers meeting. Have parents tell stories about what dating was like when they were teenagers. For fun, have parents role play what they think dating is like for teenagers today. Then have kids tell parents what dating is *really* like today. Encourage kids and parents to discuss the importance of honesty, communication and patience in dating relationships.

Dating Game—Have three guys (or girls) become contestants #1, #2 and #3. Have the contestants sit out of the view of a volunteer who'll choose one of them to "date." Tell the contestants to disguise their voices and to give serious or funny answers to the questions asked. Give the volunteer a "Dating-Game Ammo" handout (p. 48) and explain that the volunteer may ask up to four different questions (the same four for each contestant) from the handout to help choose a date.

Have fun with this game and play a number of rounds with new volunteers and contestants. Afterward, discuss how easy or difficult it was to choose someone based on just four questions. Help kids see how this game is similar to real life and how it takes time to get to know someone well. Have the winning couples go on a group date together.

PARTY PLEASER

The Dating-Exchange Party—Before the party, brainstorm ideas for safe, creative and inexpensive dates. For example, wash a friend's car together; walk through a mall and "spend" $1,000; or go to a playground and swing on the swings. Print your ideas neatly on cards and place them in unmarked envelopes. As kids arrive, randomly form "couples" for the party. Have couples enjoy a fun meal together, then blindly choose a "creative date" envelope. Have couples each follow the instructions on the card they draw and go on their creative date. Time the dates so kids can return to the church for a light snack and to talk about what they did on their dates.

If you want to encourage group dating, write the same "creative date" idea on more than one card. Then, when couples choose the same "creative date," have them go together.

The Love Retreat—Plan a weekend retreat at your church and your kids' homes. Have large group sessions at the church on Friday evening and Saturday morning. Plan to have small same-sex groups stay at kids' homes overnight during the weekend retreat.

Begin the "slumber party" section of the retreat with an intimate question-and-answer time for kids to talk with adults they trust about love, sex and dating. When kids meet at the church for the large group sessions, have them explore what the Bible says about sexuality and self-esteem. Also, plan to have fun "guys vs. girls" games to break up the evening and morning sessions. Include activities where kids can let down their guard and share openly about who they are—so they get to know each other better. Plan a fun group date for Saturday night to close the retreat.

RETREAT IDEA

Choose four questions from the following list to ask your potential "dates" during the game. Remember, you want to make a good decision about who you're going to date.

- If you could only take three things with you to a desert island, what would you take and why?
- How would you describe the other two contestants?
- Where would you go if you had all the money in the world?
- What is the perfect date?
- My faith is important to me. How would that affect our date?
- What would you buy for me if you had unlimited resources?
- Why should I choose you?
- What's the most important thing I should know about you?
- If you were an animal, what would you be and why?
- How would you describe the romantic meal we'd have on our date?
- How would you say "I love you" in your most romantic voice?
- What's the best thing you've ever done for someone else?
- What song title best describes your personality?
- Which game are you most like: Monopoly, Sorry! or Twister? Explain.